Transform your Furniture in a Weekend

Over 40 instant step-by-step makeovers

Transform your Furniture in a Weekend

Over 40 instant step-by-step makeovers

Stewart & Sally Walton

HERMES
HOUSE

First published in 2000 by Hermes House

© Anness Publishing Ltd 2000

Hermes House is an imprint of
Anness Publishing Limited
Hermes House, 88–89 Blackfriars Road, London SE1 8HA.

ISBN 1 84038 628 2

A CIP catalogue record for this book is available from the British Library

Publisher: Joanna Lorenz
Project editor: Doreen Palamartschuk
Editor: Linda Doeser
Photographers: Graham Rae, Michelle Garrett, Rodney Forte, Lucinda Symons, Peter Williams
Stylists: Leean Mackenzie, Andrea Spencer, Deena Beverley, Catherine Tully, Judy Smith,
Diana Civil
Illustrator: Madeleine David
Designer: Ian Sandom
Jacket designer: Clare Baggaley
Projects on pages 84–87 made by Andrew Gillmore

Printed in Hong Kong/China

1 3 5 7 9 10 8 6 4 2

CONTENTS

INTRODUCTION

There are many ways to furnish your home in a unique and interesting way. One method is to pay imaginative and creative designers and craftspeople to make unique and exclusive items especially for you. Another way is to let your own imagination run riot and to paint, re-cover, transform and decorate old, used furniture or cheap new pieces yourself. Not only is this a much less expensive option, it gives you the opportunity to express your own personality and reflect your lifestyle.

Most of the makeovers in this book require little in the way of special skills – just a bit of time and patience – and for those in a hurry to create a new look, there are some that are almost instant. Draped fabrics, gently distressed paint finishes and understated decoration evoke a feeling of stylish elegance. You can bring a breath of country air to the middle of the city with colourful folk art motifs, woven materials and the wonderfully easy and versatile technique of combing paint. For a crisp contemporary look, you could go for a black and white tiled table top or rejuvenate an old armchair with brilliantly coloured rubber fabric.

Create the mood and atmosphere you want, from classical to modern, at a fraction of the cost.

Most of the projects in this book are very adaptable – you can substitute a chair for a stool, bright primaries for pastel colours, flowers or fruit for a vegetable montage, a square table for a round one or a chest of drawers for a low cupboard.

The techniques are clearly explained with step-by-step instructions, so all you have to decide is where you want the motifs to appear, which patterns please you most and what colours go best with your décor. The materials required for the majority of projects are inexpensive and when you want a change, just re-cover and decorate the same pieces.

$\mathcal{O}$LD FURNITURE

Above: Turn a small, second-hand store find into a bright bedside cabinet using a palette of fresh colours and a star motif.

SECOND-HAND STORES and flea markets are wonderful sources of raw materials. Many older pieces of furniture were very well made, sometimes from attractive woods that are now concealed by an accumulation of stain, polish and grime. Look at the shape of the piece rather than its surface and if you like it and the price is right, it is worth renovating and rejuvenating. Small holes in surfaces can be filled, handles missing from drawers can be replaced and you can even replace a broken cane seat with very little effort. Preparation need not be long and arduous. If you are going to paint an old piece, it is often

Right: Try painting freehand on to a cupboard to add interest and your own style. Any cupboard or dresser doors would be suitable for this design, even modern kitchen units.

enough simply to sand the surface to provide a "key" so that the paint adheres. However, if you want to varnish or polish it or you want to add some decoration but not cover the entire surface, it is worth removing the previous finish completely. Layers of furniture polish can be washed off with vinegar diluted with warm water, but do not allow the piece to become soaked. Chemical paint and varnish strippers are very harsh and best avoided if possible as they can loosen glued joints, but sometimes using them is necessary.

Always protect your hands with rubber (latex) gloves, work in a well-ventilated area and follow the manufacturer's instructions precisely. Holes and dents can be filled with wood filler, which should be sanded smooth when dry. A wide range of handles and knobs made from metal, wood and plastic is widely available to replace missing or unattractive ones.

Above: Whether you want to give new life to an old piece of furniture or add panache to a new, plain chest of drawers, using corrugated metal lawn-edging is a modern and fresh approach.

Left: Create a flaking paint effect by using crackle-glaze medium on old cupboards or cabinets. It is perfect for those that are in need of repair.

EQUIPMENT

Above: Old, white dinner plates can be very useful for holding paint to apply to stencils and stamps.

LITTLE SPECIAL EQUIPMENT IS REQUIRED for the projects in this book, but it is worth buying high-quality paint brushes and so on to achieve the best effects.

Household paintbrushes are available in a wide range of sizes. Use one that is suitable for the size of the object you are painting. If you are using a number of colours, use separate brushes for each one. Varnishes can be applied with a paintbrush, but a special varnishing brush, which has longer bristles, will produce a smoother finish. Some projects require fine artist's or other special brushes. Buying cheap nylon versions is a false economy. Always clean brushes thoroughly after use and store them carefully.

Right: These stamps are pre-cut and are taken from Egyptian hieroglyphs. They are repeated in a regimented row to create an eye-catching pattern.

Left: Be sure to wear protective gloves when working with wire. For a professional finish, cover the edges of this chicken wire with narrow flat beading (molding).

The quantities of paint required are small in comparison with painting a room, so you will rarely need a paint kettle (pot). However, old dinner plates, preferably white and unpatterned, are useful for mixing artist's colours or holding paint for stamps or stencils.

A craft knife and self-healing cutting mat are invaluable investments. Make sure the blade you are using is very sharp. Not only will this ensure neatness and accuracy, but you are also less likely to cut yourself as blunt blades slip very easily. Similarly, ensure that scissors are strong and sharp.

A metal ruler or straight edge is best for marking out lines and is essential if you need an edge for cutting. A knife blade can catch in a wooden ruler, spoiling your work and possibly causing injury.

Below: Careful planning of your design will make execution easier and quicker.

PAINTS AND VARNISHES

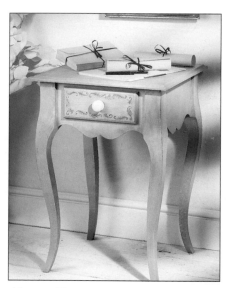

Above: If you are decorating a new table, sand the wood first with fine, grade sandpaper and apply a coat of primer. Remove the drawer knob. After applying your chosen paint colour you can distress the table by rubbing back thin layers of colour with fine wire (steel) wool.

MANY PROJECTS IN THIS BOOK use emulsion (latex) paint. This is water-soluble, easy to apply and fairly quick-drying. It gives good coverage, but it is worth remembering that two thinner coats of paint look better and are more resilient than one thick one. Emulsion paint is available in an enormous range of colours and may be matt (flat) or satin finish. Brushes can be cleaned in warm water with a little detergent, then rinsed thoroughly and shaken dry.

Artist's acrylic paints are good for applied decoration, such as stamping, stencilling and freehand painting. They are available in tubes in a vast range of colours.

Acrylic paint is flexible, easy to apply and fast-drying. As it is water-soluble, mistakes can easily be rectified while the paint is still wet. Fabric paints are available in pots and pens and may require "fixing"

Right: If you find an old table, you may have to strip off the old paint or varnish it and treat it for woodworm. Any serious holes can be filled with woodfiller and then sanded and stained to match. Emphasize the good features and play down the bad.

Left: When using découpage, make sure all the paper cut outs are stuck down flat and then you can begin to apply thin coats of shellac or clear satin varnish. You will need to apply many coats. For an even and better finish, always ensure the surface is dry before varnishing.

after they have been applied – follow the manufacturer's instructions for the best results.

Acrylic scumble is water-based and may be mixed with emulsion paint to create a semi-transparent glaze. One or two coats of varnish will protect your work. Matt varnish is often the best choice, but you can also use satin or gloss finish. It is cheaper and more thorough to apply varnish with a brush, but some types are available in spray cans.

Work in a well-ventilated room and, if using a spray, protect the surrounding area. Polyurethane varnish is a good choice for furniture, as it is durable, alcohol-resistant and heatproof to a limited extent. However, even the matt finish has a slight sheen, although it tends to "yellow" less than many other types.

Below: You can create patterns in wet paint by combing. Make a smooth combing movement into the wet varnish and then wipe the comb to prevent any build-up of varnish.

BEACHCOMBER'S STOOL

IF YOU STUMBLE ACROSS a small milking stool like this one, don't hesitate, just buy it. These sorts of stools were and still are used in kitchens, gardens and worksheds for a wide range of tasks. Small children love to sit on them and adults find them invaluable when shelves are just out of reach. They can be used for weeding, sketching, fishing or any activity that requires being close to the ground, but not actually on it. This second-hand find was painted orange before being stamped with the seashore pattern. It's just the thing to sit on while peeling shrimp or cleaning mussels.

YOU WILL NEED

small wooden stool

orange emulsion (latex) paint

household paintbrush

emulsion (latex), acrylic or poster paint: deep red, purple and pale peach

plate

foam roller

shell, seahorse and starfish stamps

matt (flat) varnish and brush

one *Paint the stool orange and leave to dry. Spread some deep red paint on the plate and run the roller through it to coat evenly. Ink the shell stamp and make a print in the centre of the stool.*

two *Ink the seahorse stamp with purple paint and make a print on each side of the shell.*

three *Ink the starfish stamp with pale peach paint. Print a starfish border overlapping the edge so that the design goes down the sides of the stool.*

four *When the paint is dry, apply a coat of varnish to the stool. This will dry to a matt (flat) sheen.*

Woven Stool Seat

MANY HOMES HAVE AT LEAST one rush stool or chair seat that would benefit from renovation, but is not worth the expense of professional attention. Rush or seagrass is not always readily available today and the notion of learning what seems to be a complex craft can be a little daunting. Instead, this simple weaving technique allows you to use rope for the seat – to great practical and visual effect. The large, blunt wooden awl is a very useful tool for this project.

YOU WILL NEED

about 36m (39yds) of 5 mm (¼in) unbleached cotton rope

craft knife

masking tape

2 wood screws

rush stool with seat removed

screwdriver

large needle

twine or strong thread

large wooden awl

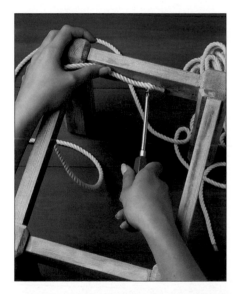

one *Divide the rope into three bundles for ease of handling. Mark each cut and bind in each place with masking tape to stop the ends fraying when you cut. Choose a screw that is long enough to go through the end of the rope and into the wood of the stool without sticking out the other side. Screw through the end of one of the rope bundles and into the centre of the first strut (strut A), on the inside of the stool.*

two *Pull the rope parallel with strut A and take it over the second strut (strut B).*

three *Take the rope all the way around strut B and then back over strut A. Maintain an even tension as you work.*

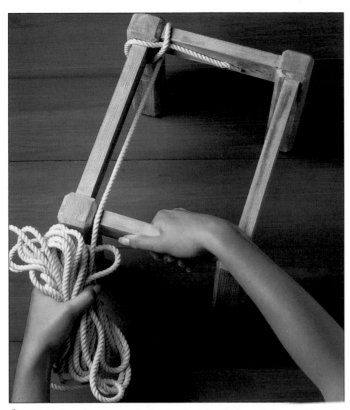

four *Bring the rope up through the middle of the stool and over the third strut (strut C).*

five *Continue working around the stool in this way, passing the rope over and around each consecutive strut until you reach the end of the first bundle.*

six *Using twine or strong thread, stitch the end of the rope securely to the adjacent piece of rope.*

seven *Wrap the end of the next bundle of rope with masking tape and stitch it in place so that it butts up to the end of the first bundle.*

➤

eight *When the short sides of the stool are complete, work the middle of the stool in a figure-of-eight, joining on more rope as necessary.*

nine *The weaving will become tighter and more difficult to work as you fill the centre. Use a large awl to create as much space as possible until no more rope can be fitted in.*

ten *Finish off the loose end of the last bundle of rope by stitching it as described in step six. Tuck the end of the rope neatly inside the weaving.*

eleven *Finally, use the awl to flatten out and neaten up any irregularities in the weaving.*

TARTAN STOOL

SIMPLE UPHOLSTERY SUCH AS THIS has been much easier since glue guns and staple guns were invented. Once you have mastered the technique shown here, you can move on to more ambitious projects. This project would work equally well on an upholstered chair seat. Give a favourite piece of furniture the tartan treatment, or look out for an old stool in a second-hand store. If the woodwork is not painted, paint it first with a white emulsion (latex) undercoat.

YOU WILL NEED

upholstered stool

medium-grade sandpaper

emulsion (latex) paint in a colour to match your tartan fabric

small decorator's brush

tartan fabric, to fit the upholstered stool top plus 2.5cm (1in) all round

staple gun

four upholstery nails

hammer

scissors

glue gun and glue sticks

upholstery braid

one *Rub down the woodwork with sandpaper. Paint with emulsion (latex), then drag over a dry paintbrush while the paint is still wet.*

two *Place the tartan fabric centrally over the upholstered stool top. Using a staple gun put a single staple in the centre of one long side. Pull the fabric taut, and then staple the opposite side in the same way.*

three *Staple the two short sides in the same way. The fabric will now be held in place by four staples.*

four *Staple along the edge of each side, placing the row of staples close together. Leave the corners open.*

five *Mitre the fabric at the corners and flatten the folds. Secure each corner temporarily. Trim the excess fabric, leaving enough to turn under a small hem and cover the corners.*

◄ **six** *Staple one mitred corner flat, turning under the small hem as you go. Remove the upholstery nail. Repeat with the opposite corner, then complete the other two corners.*

seven *Heat the glue gun. Glue one end of the braid to the bottom of the stool top at one corner. Spread a line of glue along the bottom edge. Holding the braid taut in one hand, smooth it on to the glued line with the other hand, keeping the line straight. Fold under the end of the braid at the last corner to make a neat join.* ►

DRESSING FOR DINNER

FOR VERY SPECIAL OCCASIONS, why not dress up your table and chairs? Choose a style of corsage suited to the style of your chairs. A simple unvarnished country chair, for instance, calls for understated trimmings, whereas a fancy French one requires something much more elaborate. Trim the table to match. The individual flower arrangements can be given to your guests to take home. These ideas could not be simpler, but will add to the festivities.

YOU WILL NEED

florist's wire and scissors

silk or fresh flowers

fresh greenery

2.5m (2¾yds)
organza ribbon and
scrap organza

1 cinnamon stick, pot-pourri
and star anise

fine string

glue gun and glue sticks

beads

A CHAIR WITH STYLE

one *Use florist's wire to join the flowers together at the stem. Silk ones are best because they bend.*

two *Continue binding in flowers and greenery to make an attractive corsage. Trim the stems and tuck in any ends.*

three *Finish with a ribbon bow. Make a wire hook to attach the corsage to the chair.*

LIVENING UP THE TABLE

one *Fill a teapot with pot-pourri. Then cut a circle from organza, fill it with pot-pourri and tie the top with string. Twist a cinnamon stick into the tie and tie the bag to the lid.*

two *Make a necklace for a bottle by pulling apart a piece of fine string into separate strands and glueing star anise to one strand.*

three *Decorate a decanter or jar with a piece of organza ribbon tied into bows, or threaded with beads.*

MAGIC CHAIR

COVERED IN NOVA SUEDE, this hard-backed chair has a split personality: a 1950s dining chair by day and a theatrical throne in the evening. Throws are often used to cover easy chairs, but the limitless possibilities of using them to add drama to a hard chair, totally changing its appearance, are often overlooked. Another advantage is that you can knot throws and tie them on to the uprights of a hard-backed chair and extras such as tassels or bindings can easily be incorporated.

Any fabric that is wide enough is suitable for this treatment, but soft fabrics, such as suede or velvet, are particularly stylish. Practicality is not an issue, because the covers can be whisked off to reveal the practical chair underneath.

YOU WILL NEED

hard-backed chair

large piece of plush fabric, for example, Nova suede

tassels and bindings (optional)

one *Drape the fabric over the chair, making sure it touches the ground at the front.*

two *Take up some excess fabric from the back and form a knot over both chair pegs at the back of the chair.*

three *For further embellishment, secure the corners of the fabric with tassels or bindings.*

SUPER SOFA

TRIM A PERFECTLY PLAIN sofa using only a strand of rope that curves gently down the edge of the arm and across the base. This type of decoration works extremely well in a white-on-white colour scheme because the eye is aware of the shape, but the embellishment doesn't jump out. Other types of trimming that could be used to add a stylish personal touch to your sofa are raffia edging, linen tassels and fringing.

YOU WILL NEED

sofa

graph or plain paper

pencil

rope, the length of the area
to be trimmed

clear sticky tape

scissors

dressmaker's pins

needle

strong sewing thread

one *Work out (sketch) different designs on paper for the rope to see what works the best; this style seemed sympathetic to the shape of the arm of the sofa and the lines of the seat.*

two *Bind clear sticky tape around the ends of the rope so that the ends do not fray once the rope is in position.*

three *Cut as close to the end of the tape as you can so that as little is left as possible, but it still holds the rope firmly. Pin the rope on to the sofa and hand-stitch in place.*

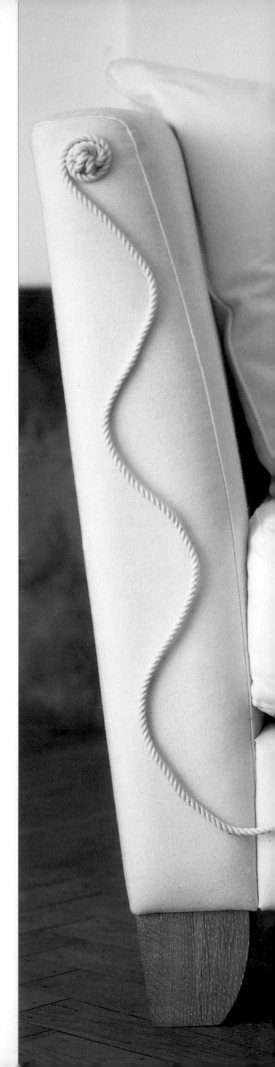

STARFISH CHAIR

OLD WOODEN CHAIRS ARE NOT expensive and, with a bit of careful hunting round second-hand stores, you should be able to find yourself a real bargain. Strip the old layers of paint – it might take some time, but it gives you a good base to work on. This chair was painted white, then it was dragged with yellow-ochre in the direction of the grain before being stamped in light grey. Choose colours that complement your bathroom scheme so that your chair will blend in.

YOU WILL NEED

medium-grade sandpaper

wooden chair

emulsion (latex) paint: white, yellow ochre and light grey

paintbrush

old plate

small roller

starfish-motif stamp

clear matt (flat) varnish

varnish brush

one *Sand the chair, then apply a coat of white emulsion (latex). Mix a thin wash of five parts water to one part yellow ochre paint. Use a dry brush to drag a little glaze at a time in the direction of the grain. Keep drying the brush as you work, to ensure you do not apply too much glaze.*

two *Spread some light grey paint on to the plate and run the roller through it until it is evenly coated. Ink the starfish stamp and print around the edge of the chair seat so that the design overlaps on to the sides.*

three *Fill in the seat area with starfish stamps, rotating the stamp to a different angle after each print. Space the stamps quite close together to make a dense pattern. Leave to dry thoroughly, then apply a coat of varnish to protect the surface.*

MINIMALIST CHAIR

SLEEK BEECH AND CHROME chairs abound in interiors magazines – with price tags to match. This makes renovating old chairs a rewarding proposition. Most second-hand office-supply stores have a host of old typist's chairs, often with torn upholstery or in ugly colours. Don't be drawn to a more modern chair that appears in a better state but has plastic-coated legs; metal legs look better when renovated.

YOU WILL NEED

old typist's chair

scissors

screwdriver or
bradawl (awl)

pliers

industrial rubber
(latex) gloves

chemical paint stripper

2.5–5cm (1–2in) brush

wire (steel) wool

soap

medium-grade sandpaper

all-in-one stain and varnish

varnish brush

wax and cloth (optional)

hammer

"domes of silence"

metal polish and soft, dry cloth

one *Start by cutting off excess fabric and foam. You need strong scissors with large plastic handles to avoid hurting your hands. Remove the fabric and the upholstery staples from the back and underside of the chair. Use the screwdriver or bradawl (awl) for getting into tricky places and the pliers to pull out the old staples.*

two *Remove the castors and any other loose parts, to prevent them being damaged by the paint stripper. Wearing the industrial rubber (latex) gloves, brush the paint stripper on the metal chair frame. Leave for 5 minutes (or as long as the manufacturer recommends) and wash off with wire (steel) wool and soapy water. Repeat until all the paint has been removed.*

three *Having removed the seat and back, make sure the surfaces are free of nails and staples. Sand the surfaces of the seat and back until smooth and clean. Seal the wood with all-in-one stain and varnish, leave to dry and wax (optional).*

four *Re-attach the seat, back and castors. Use "domes of silence" to cover any sharp bolts that might rip your clothes. Finally, polish the metal using a soft, dry cloth.*

ROPE-BOUND CHAIR

COLONIAL-STYLE AND VERANDA CHAIRS have gained considerable popularity recently but, sadly, originals are difficult to find. This is a good technique for a chair whose character would be lost if it were painted or stripped and yet which needs some form of embellishment. Natural trimmings, such as twine, rope or hessian (burlap) tape can be expensive, as you will need about 80 metres (90 yards). Look for less expensive materials, such as the sash cord used here. You could also use twine, rope or builder's scrim.

YOU WILL NEED
old chair
6 to 8 12m (12yd) bales of sash cord
glue gun

one *Starting at the back of the chair, secure the end of the cord with a small amount of glue from the gun.*

two *Begin wrapping the chair with sash cord, according to your chosen design.*

three *You can use two lengths at a time for the arms, starting with a slip knot.*

four *When you reach the end of the length, secure it by tucking it in at the back of the chair and then glue.*

POLYNESIAN THRONE

A SPLENDID ADDITION to your conservatory or log-cabin-style summer house, this chair festooned with wheat and rushes is not designed to be a mere garden seat, but a haven for sitting and musing. Gardening has become one of the most popular pastimes and garden centres are full of a huge variety of plants and garden paraphernalia. Customized garden furniture is much sought after and pricey, but you can make this stylish throne for very little, with dried grasses, craft brushes, raffia and twigs, which are available from garden centres or florists.

YOU WILL NEED

wooden chair

medium-grade sandpaper

oil-based brown paint

paintbrush

4 large bunches of wheat

large hank of raffia

double-sided tape

4 craft rush brushes

saw

staple gun

dried bamboo or rushes

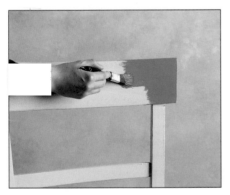

one *Sand the wooden surfaces, to provide a key for the paint. Paint the chair with the brown paint to give it a wood-grain effect. You may find it easier to remove the seat.*

two *Cover the horizontal strut of the back rest with a few lengths of wheat, tying them in place with raffia. Use the double-sided tape to hold the wheat while you work (the final attachment comes later). Attach two rush brushes diagonally, by binding the stalks to the chair frame and at the crossing point with raffia. Shorten the two remaining rush brushes to the length of the vertical chair struts.*

three *To cover the verticals of the back rest, bind them with several strands of raffia. Slot stems of wheat through the raffia until the wood is covered. Tie the shortened brushes to the front horizontals and verticals.*

four *Bind the two side brushes with many twinings of raffia. Discreetly part the brushes and secure them at the top with a few strengthening staples. Add decorative and reinforcing raffia in crisscross fashion to the back of the chair. Knot the raffia to secure it.*

five *Choose thin, flexible bamboo or rushes to bend over the top of the legs, staple in place, then bind with raffia. Staple a rough covering of wheat and rushes over the legs and horizontal struts. Knot and crisscross raffia between your turns to help it last.*

EASTERN PROMISE

DIRECTOR'S CHAIRS ARE INEXPENSIVE, but because the back rest and the seat are made of cloth they are very comfortable. Plain canvas seats are the standard form, but by customizing you can create a fun and rather chic effect. Kelim fabric is very hard-wearing and has beautiful muted colours derived from traditional carpet designs, but any fabric that is strong and without too much "give" can be used; tapestry, hessian (burlap) and sacking are all suitable. For even more character, stain the frame of the chair to match the muted tones of the kelim.

YOU WILL NEED

director's chair

wood stain and paintbrush (optional)

kelim carpet or fabric

dressmaker's pins

scissors

large darning or upholstery needle

strong darning wool (yarn)

packet of chrome poppers (at least 6)

hammer

one *Remove the old seat and back of the chair. Stain the wood of the chair, if you wish. Choose the most decorative parts of the kelim carpet or fabric and pin the old fabric to it as a pattern. Carefully cut out new seat and back pieces.*

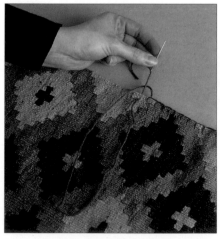

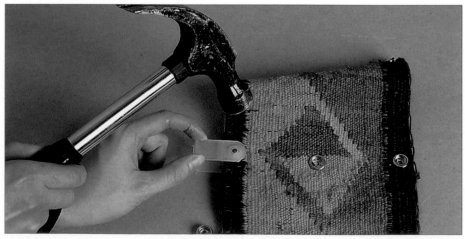

two *Thread the needle with the wool (yarn) and neatly blanket-stitch the edges to bind them.*

three *Fold over the edges of the back and fasten with chrome poppers, then slip over the uprights. Slot the seat back into position and secure firmly.*

JEWEL-BRIGHT ARMCHAIR

MANY ELEGANTLY SHAPED armchairs are disguised beneath several layers of ugly orange or dark brown varnish and dowdy upholstery fabrics. Once the covers have been removed and the old varnish has been sanded away, however, these chairs can be transformed instantly into desirable objects. Stretchy fabrics make it easier to achieve a neat, professional finish, but any upholstery fabric is suitable.

YOU WILL NEED

armchair
medium-grade sandpaper
clear wax or silicone polish
soft cloth
rubber fabric
scissors
staple gun
rubber adhesive
paintbrush
hammer
upholstery tacks
pencil
thick artist's cardboard

one *Remove all the old covers. Sand the varnish from the frame. Seal with clear wax or silicone polish. Using the existing cover pieces as patterns, cut the fabric to the size of the back rest, with a generous allowance to turn to the back surface. Stretch it over the back rest until it is hand-tight and staple it in place. Secure, in order, the top, bottom and sides, with one or two staples in the centre, before applying lines of staples to keep the fabric taut.*

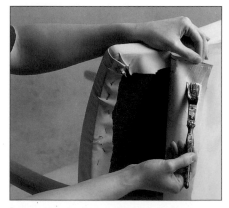

two *Cut a piece of fabric to fit the back surface of the back rest and use rubber adhesive to stick the fabric to the chair so that it covers the staples and the turned-over edges of the first layer. Hammer a tack into each corner.*

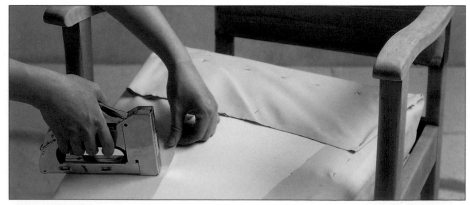

three *For the cushion, trace its shape on to the card. Cut out and staple to the cushion. Wrap the fabric around the cushion, tucking in the corners neatly, and staple to the cardboard. Attach a layer of fabric to the underside of the cushion (as in step two) using rubber adhesive.*

Sun Lounger

Sun loungers come in various heights and with all kinds of additional features, but the fabrics, which are mostly garish prints and stripes, seem at odds with the smart tubular frames. Apart from the obvious solution of re-covering, using the existing fabric as a pattern, a smart alternative is to make a textural webbing cover. This fabric is hard-wearing and overcomes the problem of sagging. Re-covered in this way, the lounger offers both comfort and durability.

YOU WILL NEED

sun lounger

chrome cleaner

soft cloth

tape measure

two x 15m (16¼yds) upholstery webbing rolls

masking tape

pencil

scissors

needle

matching thread

six packets of large eyelets

hammer

softwood block

6m (6½yds) cord or rope

one *Remove and discard the old cover. Thoroughly clean the metal frame with chrome cleaner and a soft cloth. Measure the width of the frame for the horizontal straps, and almost double this measurement so that the ends of the straps will very nearly meet in the middle.*

two *Position a couple of webbing strips with masking tape and work out how many strips you will need in each section of the frame. Cut the webbing to length and hem the ends.*

three *Follow the manufacturer's instructions for applying an eyelet to each end of the straps.*

four *Turn the lounger upside down, wrap the straps around the frame and fasten the ends together with cord or rope where they meet in the middle. Leave a gap wide enough for another strap near the hinges of the lounger.*

five *Starting at the foot, secure a vertical strap with an eyelet. Weave the strap under and over the double thickness of the horizontal straps until you reach the top. Secure the end with another eyelet.*

six *Repeat step five for all the vertical straps. Near the hinges, thread another horizontal strap through the vertical ones, but wrap the ends around the outermost verticals instead of around the frame.*

ESCHER'S DECKCHAIR

DECKCHAIRS ARE CHEAP and widely available in high-street stores in several styles. The slings are usually canvas, and come in a variety of brightly coloured plain and striped materials. Deckchair canvas comes in the correct width and with ready-sealed edges. To give an old deckchair a new lease of life use a pattern of stencils, or turn checks into a "three-dimensional" puzzle. This design is based on M.C. Escher's work and is made from a combination of contrasting motifs.

YOU WILL NEED
deckchair
deckchair canvas
fabric marker
scissors
spray adhesive
high-density foam
craft knife
self-healing cutting mat
ruler or set square
(T-square)
coloured tape
pencil
fabric paints: black and
white
paintbrush
needle
matching thread

one *Remove the old sling, making a note of how it was fastened so that you can fasten it in the same way later. Using the old cover as a pattern, cut out the new fabric, allowing for hems along the top and bottom edges.*

two *To make the two stamps for printing, photocopy the motifs from the back of the book to the desired size. Stick to the foam with spray adhesive. Cut the foam around the design with the craft knife.*

three *Using the knife, chip away the zigzag shape between the dotted lines to leave two elements of the design standing proud. Remove all the foam that is not part of the printed design. It is helpful to mark the backs of the stamps with coloured tape to indicate which colour paint is used with which stamp. Repeat steps three and four to make the other stamp.*

four *Using a ruler and pencil, draw parallel lines lengthways on the canvas, the distance between them equalling the width of the design when the two stamps are put together (see step seven).*

five *Remove the paper motifs from the stamps. Apply the black paint to the raised portion of one of the stamps.*

six *Applying light, even pressure, stamp the black design regularly within the grid lines.*

seven *Repeat with the white design. When dry, hem the top and bottom edges of the canvas, then fasten to the chair frame.*

DRAPED DIRECTOR'S CHAIR

COMPLETELY DRAPED IN a slip cover, a folding director's chair loses its functional character and takes on the role of an armchair. Avoid complicated fitting by cutting a simple tabard-type slip cover, based on squares and rectangles that are just tied together. You can then put the cover straight on to the chair without ironing, since it can be removed and stored flat when the chair is folded away.

YOU WILL NEED

director's chair
measuring tape
paper and pencil
2.5m (2¾yds) of 137cm (54in) fabric
fabric marker
set square (T-square) and ruler
scissors
dressmaker's pins
needle
matching thread
sewing machine
iron

one *Measure: (A) from floor to top edge of back; (B) from top edge of back to back of seat; (C) length of seat; (D) width of seat; (E) from centre of wooden armrest to inside base of seat; (F) from centre of armrest to floor; (G) from front edge of seat to floor.*

two *Measure and draw the pattern pieces directly on to the fabric, with a seam allowance all around each piece. Cut out, then pin, tack (baste) and sew the pieces together following the diagram at the back of the book. Press the seams and hem the raw edges.*

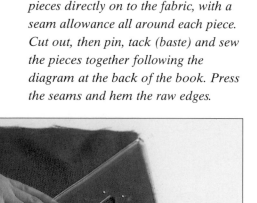

three *Mark and cut strips of fabric to make ties of a finished size of about 2.5cm (1in) wide and 40cm (16in) long. Put right sides together and sew the long edges together. Then turn them out, slip-stitch the ends and press.*

four *Sew the ties to the cover (see diagram). Slip the finished cover over the chair and knot the ties firmly.*

LACED DINING CHAIR

TRANSFORM A DULL CHAIR into a modern piece with added comfort and dramatic colour. These covers can be permanent or changed at whim. Any bright canvas fabric is suitable; economic cotton duck (canvas) has been used here. The fabric must have a little body or you will need to add a backing fabric. Ticking, linen or duck (canvas) are all suitable.

Self-covering buttons with cord loops or, for the more skilled, buttonholes, are good alternatives to lacing eyelets. Loops and toggles or frogging give a military look, especially with a bright scarlet fabric.

YOU WILL NEED

dining chair

measuring tape

foam or rubberized horse hair (to fit the back of the chair)

scissors

tape for ties

thin wadding (batting) (to fit the back of the chair)

hammer

upholstery tacks

felt-tipped pen

tissue or pattern-cutting paper

3m (3¼yds) of 130cm (51¼in) wide cotton duck (canvas)

dressmaker's pins

iron

sewing machine

matching thread

safety pins

fabric marker

hole-punching tool

hammer

eight eyelets

eyelet pliers

3m (3¼yds) cotton tape

one *Measure the chair back for the size of the foam backing or rubberized horse hair. Cut the backing to size and attach it to the chair back with ties at the top and bottom.*

two *Cover the foam or horse hair loosely with thin wadding (batting) and secure it in place with tacks.*

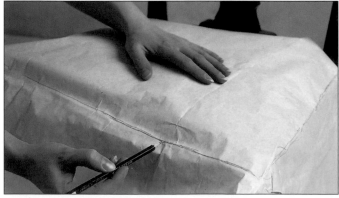

three *Lay the tissue or pattern-cutting paper on the seat and draw around it, adding a 4cm (1½in) seam allowance. Make a pattern for the front of the seat back.*

four *Decide how deep the skirt will be, then work out the dimensions for the back, which incorporates a central box pleat to allow easy removal (see diagram). Draw a pattern.*

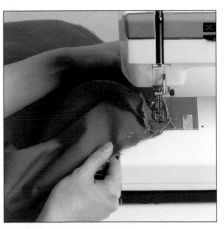

five *For the skirt, measure the two sides and front of the seat, then add 30cm (12in) for each of the four box pleats. Add 4cm (1½in) to the depth as a seam allowance. Make a pattern.*

six *Lay the patterns on your material and cut out each piece. Take the back panel and pin the central box pleat down to 4cm (1½in) from the top of the seat and press it.*

seven *Stitch the front panel to the top of the seat panel with the right sides together. Trim and press open all the seams as you go.*

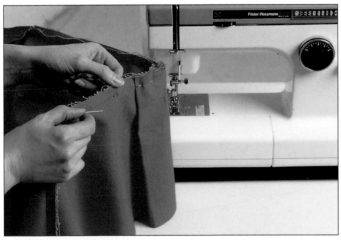

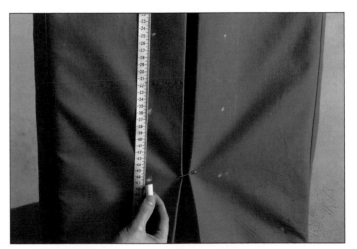

eight *Stitch the front panel to the back at the top and sides. Hem the bottom edge of the skirt and back. Fold, pin and press the box pleats so they fall in the corners of the seat. Machine stitch the seat and skirt in place along the top edges.*

nine *Put the cover on the chair, close the central back pleat with safety pins and mark the positions of the eyelets with a fabric marker.*

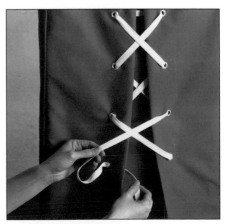

ten *Remove the cover. Using a hole-punching tool and hammer, make holes for the eyelets.*

eleven *Following the manufacturer's instructions, attach the eyelets.*

twelve *Put the cover on the chair and lace up the back with cotton tapes.*

➤

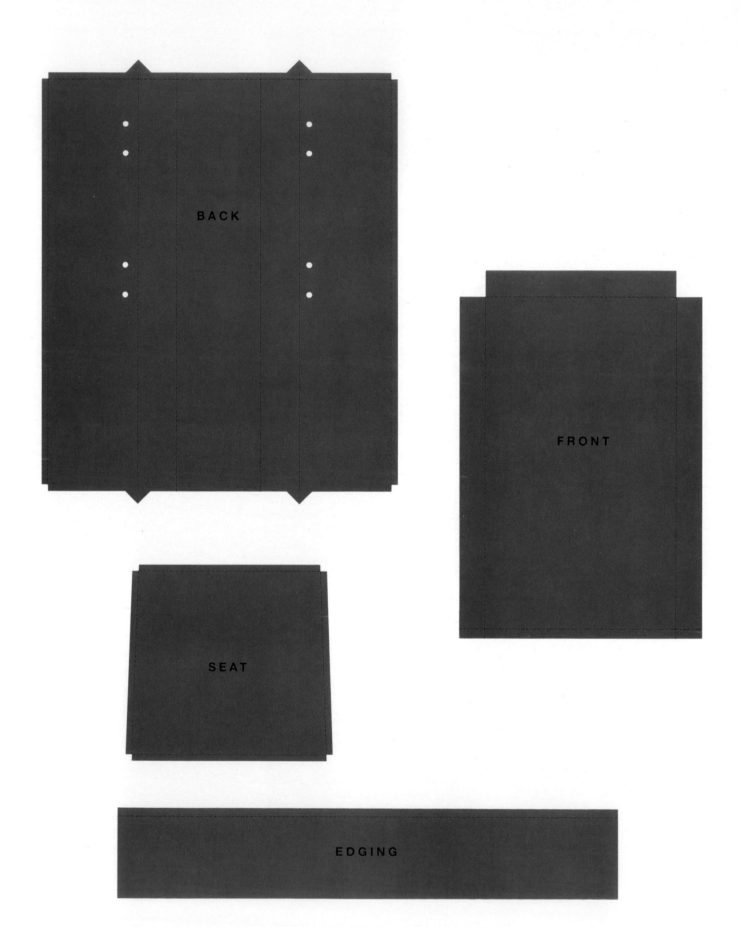

SHEER FABRIC CHAIR

 A BEAUTIFUL CHAIR with wonderful curved legs, a ladder back and cane seat might not seem to need further treatment; yet sometimes, for a change, or for a special occasion, such as a wedding party or a Valentine's Day dinner, you might want to decorate a chair without masking its integral beauty. A wistful, romantic appeal can be given by swathing the chair in translucent fabric to give it a softness which looks very special. The transparent fabric could be coloured or use one of the metallic fabrics in gold or silver, so long as the bones of the chair show through. Tie the sash that takes up the extra fabric in a knot or a big, soft bow and leave it either at the back or on the seat, like a cushion.

YOU WILL NEED

wooden chair

tissue or pattern-cutting paper

pencil

dressmaker's pins

3m (3¼yds) of 137cm (54in) transparent silk, voile or organza

fabric marker

dressmaker's scissors

measuring tape

sewing machine, matching thread and iron

one *Trace the shape of the chair back rest. Use this as a template for cutting the back and front of the back rest cover, adding 2cm (¾in) all round for seams. Pin the template to the fabric, draw around it and cut out the pieces. Trace the shape of the seat in the same way. Transfer on to fabric, adding 2cm (¾in) for seams. Measure from the seat edge to the floor, for the depth of the skirt. Add 2cm (¾in) for seams.*

two *For the skirt, add 120cm (48in) to the circumference of the chair seat. Cut as one panel.*

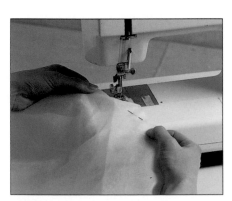

three *For the sash, allow 2m (2yds) x 40cm (16in). Right sides facing, stitch the bottom of the front back rest panel to the back of the seat panel.*

four *Press open all the seams as you go. With right sides together, stitch the front back rest panel to the back.*

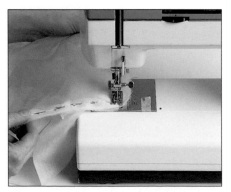

five *Hem bottom of skirt. Press, pin pleats. Hem top of skirt. Sew to seat panel at sides and front and to back panel at back. Fold sash in half, right sides together. Sew seams. Turn right sides out, stitch open end. Tie to chair.*

WILD WEST CHAIR

IF YOU HAVE AN old armchair of these robust proportions, it will lend itself to this fun treatment reminiscent of the pioneer days of the Old West. Make it over with animal-skin prints and leather fringing for a new and imaginative look, as well as a cosy and comfortable feel. You could also use leatherette for the cushion covers or blankets, which would still be in keeping with this masculine look.

YOU WILL NEED
armchair
fun-fur or animal-skin fabric
upholstery needle
strong thread
tape measure
suede or leather
ruler
craft knife
self-healing cutting mat
PVA (white) leather glue
double-sided tape
pencil
softwood block
studs
hammer
rubber or softwood scrap

one *Remove the seat cushions of the armchair and wrap in fun-fur or animal-skin fabric, leaving sufficient fabric to make a continuous flap the length of the cushion. Stitch securely. Decide on the length of fringing needed to decorate the inside and outside edges of the arms of the chair.*

two *Decide how deep you want the fringe on the leather or suede to be. Measure and cut the fringe with a craft knife on a cutting mat, leaving sufficient uncut material to make a hem. Apply PVA (white) glue to the edge of the leather or suede and fold over the hem. Press it down firmly.*

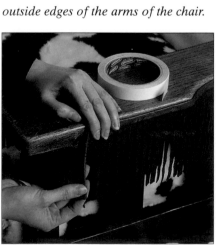

three *Apply double-sided tape to the chair arms and stick on the fringing, matching it on both arms.*

four *Mark the positions of the studs with a pencil, using a block of wood to gauge the distance between each. Position the studs with your thumb, press gently and then tap with a hammer, protecting the stud with a scrap of rubber or softwood.*

ROBOT CHAIR

A SIMPLE CHAIR MAY not suit a dramatic paint treatment, but you can add to basic chairs to create more height or add drama with a ladder-back effect. The easiest addition to use is already turned dowel, available from builders' merchants and DIY shops, which should be the thickness of your drill bit. If you are prepared for extra work in drilling out larger holes, all kinds of struts could be used, including twisted and carved pieces of the types used for shelving or balustrades. Decorating the chair with computer-age motifs adds further impact.

YOU WILL NEED

ladder-back chair
pencil
drill, with wood drill bit
ruler or measuring tape
saw
wooden dowels
medium-grade sandpaper
hammer
royal blue emulsion (latex) paint
medium and fine paintbrushes
acrylic paint: white, fluorescent yellow, green and pink
permanent black marker
clear matt (flat) varnish
varnish brush

one *Mark the positions of the holes for the dowels. Drill all the holes. Keep the drill straight, or the dowel won't pass through both holes. Measure the back of the chair. Cut the dowels slightly longer than the chair back and sand the ends.*

two *Pass the dowel through one upright of the chair and line it up with the hole on the second upright.*

three *With a hammer, lightly tap the dowel through the second hole. Leave an equal amount of dowel showing on either side. Paint the whole chair with a blue base coat. Long, slow, even strokes will produce an even finish.*

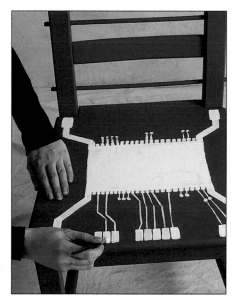

four *With a fine brush and white paint, sketch the outline for the "computer chip" design on the chair seat and on the wide struts of the back. The white provides a good base for the fluorescent paint. Again, with a fine brush, paint on the design in yellow, green and pink fluorescent paints.*

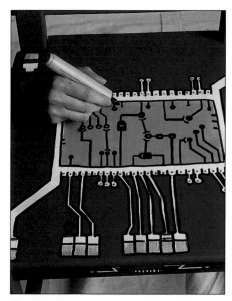

five *Outline the design with the marker and add any further detail. Finally, to protect all the paintwork, coat the whole chair with clear varnish.*

PAINTED TABLE

IT IS STILL POSSIBLE TO FIND bargain tables in second hand stores and this one cost less than a tenth of the price of a new one. It is the sort of table that you imagine standing in a country cottage parlour, covered with a lace-edged cloth and laden with tea-time snacks. There is no guarantee that you will find a similar table, but any old table could be decorated in the same way.

one *Prepare and treat the table, as necessary, filling any serious holes with wood filler and staining to match. Use a cloth to rub the dark wood-stain into the table legs, applying more as it is absorbed into the wood. The finish should be an even, almost black tone.*

two *Paint the base of the table top with red emulsion (latex).*

three *Measure 5cm (2in) from the edge of the table and place a strip of masking tape this distance in from each edge. Leave a 2cm (¾in) gap and place strips of masking tape to run parallel with the first set.*

four *Fill in the strip between the tapes with the green paint and leave to dry.*

five *Apply two coats of shellac to the table, leaving each to dry thoroughly. Finish the table with a coat of beeswax polish, buffing it to a warm sheen with a soft clean cloth.*

EGYPTIAN TABLE TOP

THE BEAUTY OF THIS TABLE-TOP design lies in its simplicity. Just one colour was used on a bold blue background, with three similar images stamped in regimented rows. The table used here has a lower shelf, but the design would work equally well on an occasional table. The salmon-pink prints show up well on the rich background, making it look even bluer. The stamps are pre-cut and are taken from Egyptian hieroglyphs. The finished table could be the surprising and eye-catching centrepiece of a room decorated in subdued colours.

YOU WILL NEED

3 hieroglyph rubber stamps

ruler and set square (T-square)

2 cardboard strips, one the length and one the width of the table, for guides

felt-tipped pen

salmon pink emulsion (latex) or acrylic paint

small paint roller

piece of plastic

one *Use the stamps and ruler to measure out the stamp positions. Place a cardboard strip along the edge of the table and mark as many stamp lengths as will fit along, leaving even spaces between them. Mark stamp widths along the second strip.*

two *Position the card strips at 90 degrees to each other to mark the position of the first row. Coat the roller evenly with paint on a piece of plastic.*

three *Coat the hieroglyphs and stamp in sequence along the first row.*

four *Move the wide strip up one stamp space on the short strip, check that it is at 90 degrees and stamp a second row. Continue until the table is covered.*

VEG-TABLE

A SMALL TABLE will fit in anywhere – in the living room, the hallway, the kitchen, the patio or the conservatory. These chilli peppers make a colourful decoration for a table with an easily achieved distressed paint finish. Experiment with different paint colours and decorate with your favourite fruits or vegetables.

YOU WILL NEED

wooden table

emulsion (latex) paint:
white, green and yellow

large and medium
household paintbrushes

soft cloth

wax

fine-grade sandpaper

tape measure

colour pictures of vegetables

craft knife

self-healing cutting mat

small, sharp scissors

piece of plastic

PVA (white) glue

clear water-based acrylic
satin varnish

varnish brush

one *Apply a coat of white paint to the table and leave to dry. Apply a coat of green emulsion (latex) to the table and leave to dry.*

two *Using a soft cloth, rub wax unevenly over the surface of the table and leave to dry.*

three *Apply a coat of the yellow emulsion to the table and leave to dry.*

four *Using fine-grade sandpaper, gently rub the surface of the table until you can see the green paint showing through. Sand the surface until the desired distressed look is achieved.*

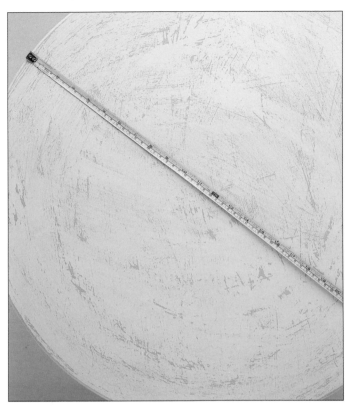

five *Measure the table top so that you know by how much to enlarge the vegetables. You may find it helpful to make a newspaper pattern so that you can estimate how many photocopies are required.*

six *Photocopy the vegetable pictures. Start by cutting out the small inner areas of the vegetable design using a craft knife and cutting mat.*

seven *Cut out larger pieces with a small pair of scissors, taking care not to break the delicate stems.*

eight *Arrange the vegetables and leaves on the table until you are happy with the design.*

➤

nine *One by one, turn the cut-outs upside down on a piece of plastic and apply the glue. Gently place them back in position, carefully smoothing the surface and making sure there are no creases.*

ten *Varnish the table top with at least four coats of clear satin varnish, leaving each coat to dry before applying the next.*

SCANDINAVIAN TABLE

THIS PRETTY LITTLE TABLE has been distressed by rubbing back thin layers of colour with fine wire (steel) wool. Focusing on the areas that would normally suffer most from general wear and tear gives an authentic aged look. The simple leaf design is painted freehand and picked out with paler highlights. If you are decorating a new wooden table, sand the wood first with fine-grade sandpaper and apply a coat of primer. Remove the drawer knob.

YOU WILL NEED

MDF (medium-density fiberboard) or wooden table with drawer

rubber (latex) gloves

fine wire (steel) wool

emulsion (latex) paint: dark yellow, grey-green, white, dark and medium-green and pale green

flat artist's paintbrush

small household paintbrushes

acrylic scumble

fine artist's paintbrush

clear matt (flat) acrylic varnish and brush

one *Rub down the table with fine wire (steel) wool, wearing a pair of rubber (latex) gloves. Pay particular attention to the bevelled edges.*

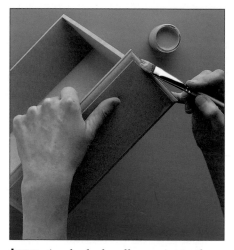

two *Apply dark yellow paint to the mouldings, if any, around the edge of the drawer and the table top.*

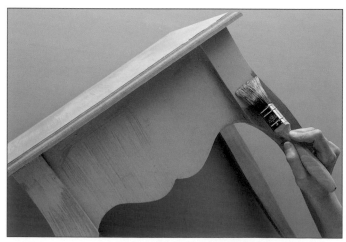

three *Apply two coats of grey-green paint to the rest of the table and the drawer front, leaving it to dry between coats.*

four *Wearing rubber (latex) gloves, rub down the entire surface of the table with wire (steel) wool.*

five *Combine equal quantities of white paint and scumble. Apply sparsely to the green areas with a dry brush, using light diagonal strokes and varying the angle of the brush to give an even coverage.*

six *Combine equal quantities of dark yellow paint and scumble. Paint this over the moulding.*

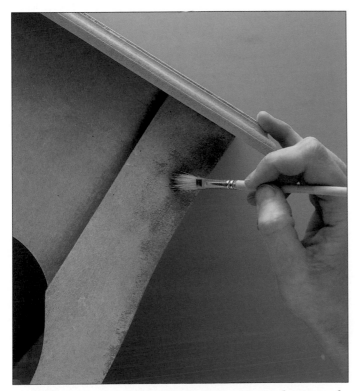

seven *Apply light dabs of dark green paint to the parts of the table that would receive the most wear: the top corners of the legs and underneath. Leave to dry, then rub back with wire (steel) wool.*

eight *Paint a scrolling leaf design around the edge of the drawer front in pale green. Pick out the stalks and leaf veins with fine brushstrokes in medium green.*

➤

nine *Still using the fine artist's paintbrush, add white and yellow highlights to the leaf design.*

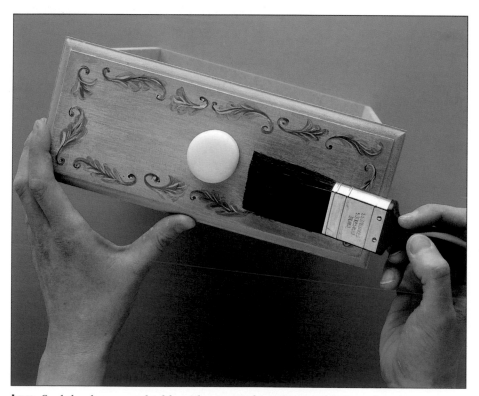

ten *Seal the drawer and table with a coat of acrylic varnish for protection.*

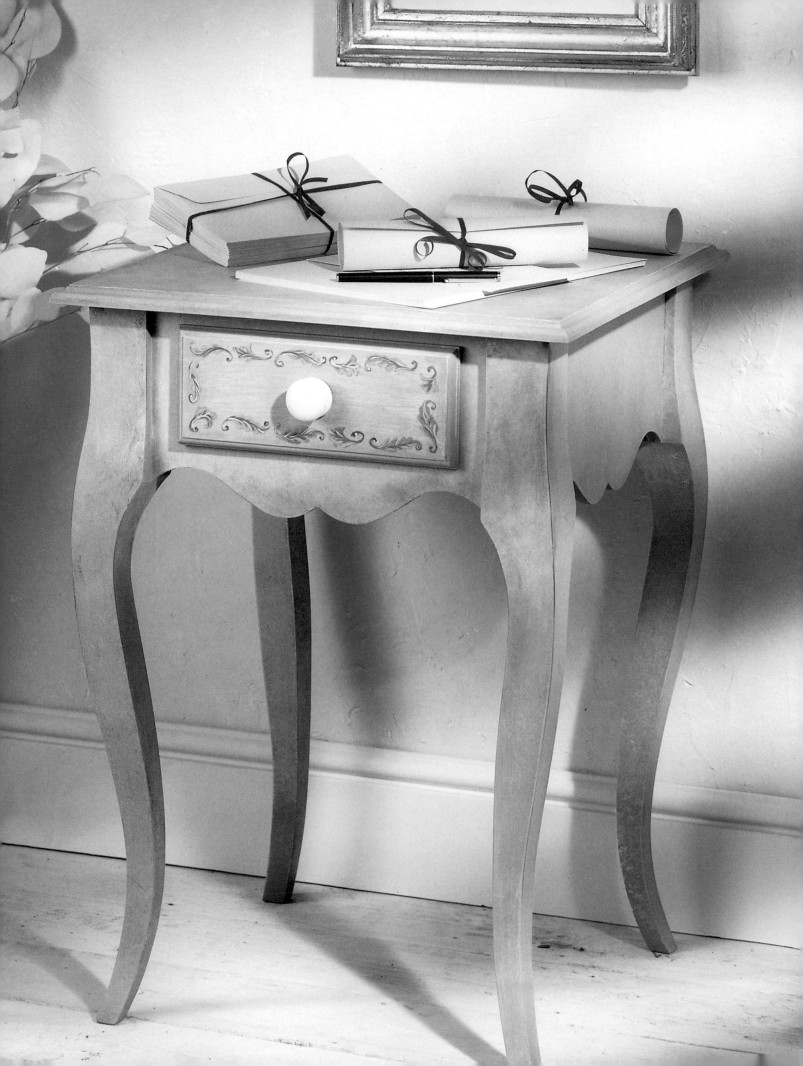

BLACK AND WHITE TABLE

BLACK AND WHITE TILED PATHS, porches and hallways are a familiar sight in town houses and they prove the age-old design theory that simplicity is best. There is something immensely pleasing about the simple regularity of black and white patterns, whether the tiles are set chequerboard style or as diamonds. There are many possible variations on the design shown here; the border could be wider or set out in one colour only. It should be noted that these tiles are not the heavy tessellated flooring type, but a lighter variety that is easier to cut manually.

YOU WILL NEED

small table

diluted PVA (white) glue

glue brush

craft knife

pencil and ruler

hand saw

thin wooden batten

panel pins (brads)

wood glue

tack hammer

protective leather gloves
and goggles

tile cutter

small black and white tiles

rubber (latex) gloves

notched spreader

all-in-one flexible tile
adhesive and grout

sponge

emulsion (latex) paint and
paintbrushes (optional)

one *Seal the bottom and top of the table top with a coat of diluted PVA (white) glue. When dry, scuff the surface with a craft knife as a key.*

two *Draw lines from corner to corner and between the centre points of each side as guides.*

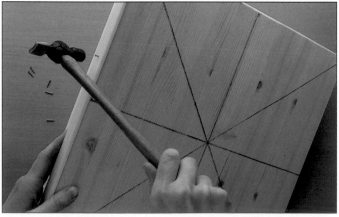

three *Cut four lengths of wooden batten to fit around the edges of the table. Attach with wood glue and panel pins (tacks), leaving a lip around the top edge exactly the depth of the tiles.*

four *Draw border lines around the edges. Wearing leather gloves and goggles, cut a few tiles diagonally to make triangles. Lay these out as a border on the table top and fill in with whole tiles to see how many will fit.*

◄ **five** *Wearing rubber (latex) gloves, spread tile adhesive over the surface of the table top, inside the border lines. Starting with the triangular border tiles, set out the pattern, butting the tiles together and leaving very small gaps for grouting.*

six *Wearing leather gloves and goggles, cut strips of tile to fit around the borders, then set in place as before. Once the tiles have dried, grout the surface, removing any excess with a damp sponge. Seal and paint the sides and legs of the table if required.* ➤

PAINTED CHEST

UP UNTIL THE **18**TH CENTURY, it was the custom for country brides to take their own decorated linen chests into their new homes, especially in northern Europe and Scandinavia. The dowry chest was often made by the bride's father, who lovingly carved and painted it as a farewell gift to his daughter. Marriage customs accounted for many rural crafts, and the family took great pride in providing a handsome chest for a bride. This custom was continued among the first settlers in North America.

YOU WILL NEED
blanket chest

shellac and brush (optional)

Emulsion (latex) paint: dusky blue and regency cream

household paintbrushes

tracing paper

pencil

pair of compasses (compass)

ruler

"Antique Pine" acrylic varnish

graining comb

clean cloths

one *If you are starting with bare wood, apply a coat of shellac to seal the surface. When dry, apply a coat of dusky blue paint to the chest. Trace and enlarge the pattern from the template section and use it as a guide to position the panels. Draw the panels with a pair of compasses (compass) and ruler.*

three *Apply a thick coat of varnish to one panel only. Quickly comb the varnish in a pattern, following the shape of the panel. Make one smooth combing movement into the wet varnish and then wipe the comb to prevent any build-up of varnish. Complete one panel before repeating with the next panel.*

two *Fill in all the panels with cream paint and leave to dry.*

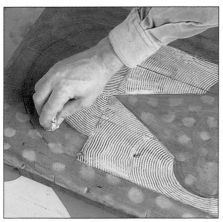

four *Apply a coat of varnish to the whole chest. Immediately take a just-damp cloth, screw it into a ball and use it to dab off spots of the varnish.*

MINIBUS TOYBOX

EVERY CHILD SHOULD BE ENCOURAGED to put away his or her toys at the end of the day. This eye-catching toybox might just do the trick! The pastel-coloured patches behind the bus stamps give the box a 1950s look. These are stencilled on to a light turquoise background. Stamp the buses on randomly so that some extend beyond the background shapes. Keep changing the angle of the stamp – the effect will become almost three-dimensional.

YOU WILL NEED

hinged wooden box

emulsion (latex) paint: turquoise and three pastel colours

paintbrushes

stencil card (stock) and scalpel

4 plates and 2 rollers

brown stamping ink and minibus stamp

one *Apply two coats of turquoise (latex) emulsion paint. Cut out the background stencil. It should be large enough for the whole stamp.*

two *Spread the three pastel-coloured paints on plates. Roll the first colour through the stencil on to the box. You need a shape for each colour. Wash the roller and apply the two remaining colours, painting through the stencil as before. Balance the shapes with an equal amount of background colour. Leave to dry.*

three *Pour some brown ink on to a plate. Coat the rubber stamp with the ink using a rubber roller. Stamp the bus motif on to the pastel background patches.*

four *Allow the stamps to overlap the patches and vary the angle.*

BLANKET CHEST

YOU CAN ALMOST GUARANTEE that every interesting pine chest has been discovered by now, stripped and sold for a profit, but there are still solid work chests that can be used as a good base for this project. The blanket used for covering the chest is the utilitarian sort used by furniture removal firms as a protective wrapping. Any blanket would be suitable, but this sort has lots of "give" because of the way it is woven and so can be stretched for a smooth fit. The chest has a piece of upholstery foam on it so it doubles up as a comfortable bedroom seat. The lid is held down by a leather strap – suitcase straps or old horse tack are ideal, as they come in longer lengths than leather belts.

YOU WILL NEED

wooden chest

screwdriver

pliers

tape measure

blanket

dressmaker's scissors

staple gun

upholstery foam, to fit lid

ruler

craft knife and cutting mat

upholstery tacks

small hammer

piece of leather (or cardboard)

scrap cardboard

leather strap

one *Unscrew and remove the hinges from the lid and remove any protruding nails or screws. Measure around the chest for the length of the blanket. Then measure the height of the chest. Double the height and add 13cm (5in).*

two *Cut the blanket to size. Spread it out, and lay the chest on its front in the middle with an even amount of blanket either side and 8cm (3in) below the base. Cut from the front edge of the blanket, in a straight line, to the left and right front corners of the chest. Staple the cut section inside the chest.*

three *Smooth the blanket down the front and staple it under the base. Cover the rest of the chest in the same way. Fold the blanket round from both sides to meet at the back, and staple it in place. Staple all the lining neatly inside.*

four *Cut a piece of blanket about 10cm (4in) larger than the lid on all sides. Place the foam in the middle of the blanket with the lid on top. Press down the foam, pull up the blanket on one side and staple it in place.*

five *Cut a triangular section off each corner. Leave enough blanket to fold up and staple to the lid. Fold the cut edge up and staple it across the corner.*

◄ **six** *Staple the side pieces over the first. Neaten by folding and trimming. Work on diagonal corners of the chest alternately.*

seven *Trim the chest, and secure the fastening strap to the lower half with upholstery tacks. Use a cardboard strip as a guide to keep the spacing even.* ➤

CHICKEN-WIRE CUPBOARD

CHICKEN WIRE GIVES A RUSTIC LOOK and is very practical in a pantry or kitchen. The deep red paintwork is covered with a darker glaze that is combed while it is still wet. Combing is a traditional technique, popular with folk artists and country furniture makers. This style is full of vitality, so be bold and enjoy making patterns. Choose a cupboard with a panelled wooden door. It's easy to tap away any beading (molding) around each panel, then tap around the edge of the panel to free it from the door. For a professional finish, cover the edges of the chicken wire with narrow flat beading.

YOU WILL NEED

small wooden cupboard with panelled door

medium- and fine-grade sandpaper

acrylic paints: deep red, raw umber and ultramarine

medium household paintbrushes

craft knife

self-healing cutting mat

small piece of mounting (mat) board or firm cardboard

old white plate and old knife or spatula for mixing

PVA (white) glue

cloth

antiquing varnish and brush

tape measure

12mm (½in) chicken wire

wire-cutters

small hammer and small staples or staple gun

one *Remove the door panels and sand all over the woodwork with medium-grade sandpaper. Then sand the cupboard again, this time using fine-grade sandpaper.*

two *Paint the cupboard inside and out with deep red acrylic paint.*

three *Using the craft knife, cut small V-shaped "teeth" along one edge of the mounting (mat) board or cardboard to make the comb.*

four *Mix a purple brown using all three colours. Mix this with the same quantity of PVA (white) glue to make a glaze. Using a separate brush, brush the glaze over the deep red paint. Comb it before the glue becomes tacky. Wipe the comb clean each time you lift it.*

five *The glaze looks milky when wet, but will dry clear. When the glaze is dry, apply a coat of antiquing varnish with a clean brush.*

◄ **six** *Measure each door panel and add 2.5cm (1in) all around. Cut chicken wire to fit and trim any sharp edges with wire-cutters.*

seven *Using a hammer and staples or a staple gun, staple the wire to the back of the door. Start by stapling one long side, then one end. Pull the wire taut, then staple the other two sides.* ➤

SEASIDE KITCHEN CUPBOARD

BRING THE LOOK OF HAPPY seaside vacations into your kitchen throughout the year. This effect is ideal for painting on to cupboards or cabinets that are in need of repair and attention. The flaking paint on the cupboard is the result of applying a crackle-glaze medium between the two layers of colour.

YOU WILL NEED

emulsion (latex) paint in
medium blue and white
paintbrush
cupboard
household paintbrush
crackle-glaze medium

one *Apply two base coats of medium blue emulsion (latex) paint to the outside of the cupboard. Leave to dry.*

two *When the blue paint is dry, apply a good coat of crackle-glaze medium to the centre panel, following the manufacturer's instructions.*

three *Paint a good coat of white emulsion over the area where you applied the crackle-glaze medium. Do not overbrush, since the medium will react with the paint fairly quickly to produce the crackle effect.*

four *Complete the surround to the cupboard panel by scraping the excess white paint from the brush and pulling along the edging in the direction of the grain of the wood.*

STARRY CABINET

TURN A SMALL, SECOND-HAND STORE FIND into a unique bedside cabinet using a palette of fresh colours and a star motif. Before you start to paint, divide the piece visually into blocks, each of which will be a different colour, with a further shade for the frame. Keep all the colours in similar tones to achieve this pretty, sugared-almond effect.

YOU WILL NEED

medium-grade sandpaper

wooden cabinet

wood filler (optional)

acrylic wood primer

medium and fine household paintbrushes

emulsion (latex) paint: green, pink, blue and yellow

wooden knobs

star rubber stamp

stamp inkpads in a variety of colours

drill and drill bit

screwdriver and screws

masking tape

acrylic spray varnish

one *Sand the cabinet to remove any rough patches, old paint or varnish. Fill any holes with wood filler and sand down. Apply a coat of primer and leave to dry.*

two *Paint the cabinet using different coloured emulsion (latex) paints and allow to dry.*

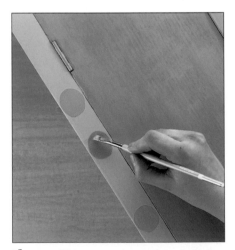

three *Using an assortment of all the colours, except that of the frame, paint a row of spots around the frame.*

four *Paint the wooden knobs and, when the paint has dried, stamp a contrasting star motif on each one using coloured inkpads. When dry, drill screw holes and screw the knobs into position.*

five *Stamp a contrasting star motif on to each of the spots around the cabinet frame.*

◄ **six** *Use masking tape to mark out a row of stripes along the bottom of the cabinet and paint them in a contrasting colour.*

seven *When all the paint is dry, spray with a coat of acrylic spray varnish and leave to dry thoroughly.*

►

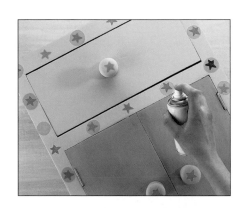

SHELL DRAWER KNOBS

THIS SIMPLE PROJECT TRANSFORMS a plain set of wooden drawers into an eye-catching piece of furniture. The distressed paintwork finish is easier to achieve than it looks and gives the chest of drawers a subtly aged appearance that works well in combination with the shells. Extend the shell theme to make door knobs for cupboards and wardrobes in exactly the same way but using larger shells and screws.

YOU WILL NEED

protective gloves

epoxy putty

six cockle (or scallop) shells

six screws

small chest of drawers

emulsion (latex) paint: two
shades of green

paintbrush

candle

wire (steel) wool

saw

bamboo cane

drill

one *Wearing protective gloves, combine the two parts of the epoxy putty and fill the backs of the shells with it. Embed the heads the screws in the putty as deeply as possible. Leave to dry.*

two *Paint the chest of drawers with the darker shade of green paint and leave to dry.*

three *Run over the painted surface of the chest of drawers randomly with the candle to give the second coat of paint a mottled effect.*

four *Paint the chest of drawers with the lighter shade of green paint and leave to dry.*

five *Rub the paintwork with wire (steel) wool to expose the undercoat in places. At the edges, rub down to the wood for a distressed look.*

six *Saw six 1 cm (½ in) lengths of bamboo. Thread a piece of bamboo on to the screw embedded inside each shell. Drill a hole in the front end of each drawer and screw on the knobs.*

PUNCHED-PANEL CABINET

TIN-PANELLED FURNITURE gives a clean, modern look, and this simple flower motif in aluminium will invest a room with new energy. Transform a bathroom cabinet or small cupboard by removing the centre panel from the door and replacing it with a punched-aluminium panel.

YOU WILL NEED

small wooden cabinet with panelled door

ruler

pencil

aluminium sheet

protective gloves

tin snips (shears or clippers)

paper

adhesive tape

protective pad

centre punch

hammer

panel pins (brads)

one *Remove the centre panel from the cabinet door and measure the rebated area to establish the size of the metal panel.*

two *Transfer the measurements to the aluminium and cut using the tin snips (shears or clippers).*

three *Trace around the metal panel on a sheet of paper, then draw your design: in this case, a symmetrical flower.*

four *Tape the paper pattern securely to the metal panel. Working on a protective pad, punch around the outlines of the design using a centre punch and hammer.*

◄ **five** *Remove the paper pattern, turn the panel over and punch from the other side to "raise" a section of your design: in this case, the centre of the flower. Work from the outside of the design to the centre.*

six *Attach the panel into the door by tapping a panel pin (brad) into each corner of the frame on the inside, taking care not to mark the metal. Neaten the inside by applying tape around the edge of the panel.* ➤

METAL-FACED DRAWERS

WHETHER YOU WANT to jazz up an old piece of furniture or add panache to a new, plain chest of drawers, corrugated metal lawn-edging is perfect for the job. Simply find the most suitable width, cut it to size and screw it to the drawer fronts.

YOU WILL NEED
tape measure
set of drawers
metal lawn-edging strip
tin snips (shears or clippers)
protective gloves
scrap board
drill and drill bits
permanent marker
screws
screwdriver
drawer handles or knobs

one *Measure the drawer fronts and cut the lawn-edging to size using tin snips (shears or clippers).*

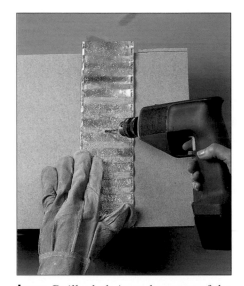

two *Drill a hole in each corner of the metal strips and also in the centre for the handle.*

three *Lay the metal strip on the front of the drawer and mark the positions of the drilled holes.*

four *Drill the four corners of the drawer front.*

five *Using the four drilled holes, screw the metal strip to the front of the drawer.*

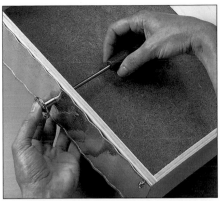

six *Finally, attach a decorative handle to the centre front of each drawer.*

PAWPRINT SHELVES

THIS SIMPLE PAINT EFFECT is based on the traditional "pawprint" pattern – the more naive and informal it looks, the better. The decoration is applied very simply with a piece of sponge to give an all-over, random effect. This technique could be used on another piece of wooden furniture, such as a cupboard or chair.

YOU WILL NEED

old wooden shelf unit

fine-grade sandpaper

acrylic paint: golden ochre and Venetian red

old white plate

small decorator's brushes

small piece of sea sponge

pencil

no. 2 lining brush

PVA (white) glue

one *Sand the shelf unit. Pour some golden ochre paint on to a plate. Paint the shelf unit and then leave to dry.*

two *Add some Venetian red paint to darken the colour. Dip a small piece of sponge in the mixture and apply in spots all over the unit. Leave to dry.*

three *Using a pencil, mark a line all around the top of the shelf unit. Rest the point of the pencil on the front, keeping your other fingers rigid, then run the pencil along to give an even line.*

four *Using a lining brush, carefully go over the pencil line with Venetian red paint. Support your painting hand to keep it steady. Leave to dry.*

◄ **five** *Pour some PVA (white) glue on to a plate and mix on a brushful of Venetian red paint to make a slightly tinted glaze. The glue is milky when wet but will be clear when dry.*

six *Using a separate brush, paint the glaze over the shelf unit. There is no need to varnish, as the glue will protect the surface.* ➤

SCANDINAVIAN PANELS

PAINTED FURNITURE IS VERY POPULAR in Scandinavia, especially designs celebrating nature. These beautiful panels are painted freehand with flowing brushstrokes. Don't worry too much about making the doors symmetrical – it is more important that the painting should look natural. Practise the strokes with both brushes first on a piece of paper until you feel confident. Any cupboard or dresser doors would be suitable for this design, even modern kitchen units.

YOU WILL NEED

cupboard

pale yellow ochre emulsion (latex) paint

medium household paintbrush

pencil

artist's acrylic paint: yellow ochre, ultramarine and white

old white plates

no. 3 lining brush

no. 8 rounded watercolour brush

clear matt (flat) varnish and brush

one *Paint the door panels with pale yellow ochre emulsion (latex) and leave to dry. Draw the design on each panel in pencil, using the template at the back of the book as a guide.*

two *Put some yellow ochre artist's acrylic paint on to a plate. Mix in ultramarine to make grey-green. Using the lining brush, begin painting the design at the top of the first panel.*

three *Work your way down the panel, resting your painting hand on the other hand to keep it steady.*

four *Put some white acrylic paint on to a plate. Mix in yellow ochre to make cream. Using the watercolour brush, paint the flowerpot and swirls below. Add the flowers, applying pressure to the brush. Darken the paint with more yellow ochre, then add the soil.*

five *Paint the other panel and leave to dry. Apply a protective coat of clear matt (flat) varnish.*

PAINTED DRESSER

IF THERE IS ONE ITEM that typifies country style in most people's minds, it must surely be the dresser. A sturdy base cupboard topped with china-laden shelves is an irresistible sight. It doesn't have to be custom-made – it could easily be a chest of drawers combined with a set of bookshelves. The trick is to make sure that the two are balanced visually with the height and depth of the shelves suiting the width of the base. The washed-out paint effect is achieved by using no undercoat and rubbing the dried paint back to the wood with sandpaper and wire (steel) wool.

YOU WILL NEED

dresser or combination of shelves and base cupboard

shellac

household paintbrushes

emulsion (latex) paint: light blue, dark red (optional) and cream

household candle (optional)

wire (steel) wool

medium-grade sandpaper

"Antique Pine" varnish and brush

one *Apply a coat of shellac to the dresser to seal the bare wood. Leave to dry, then apply a coat of blue paint following the direction of the grain. Leave to dry.*

two *If desired, rub candle wax along the edges of the dresser before applying a coat of red paint. The wax will prevent the second colour from adhering completely and will create a distressed effect.*

three *Apply a coat of red paint, then paint the backing boards with cream paint, following the direction of the grain.*

four *When the paint is dry, use wire (steel) wool and medium-grade sandpaper to rub back to bare wood along the edges to simulate wear and tear.*

five *Finally, apply a coat of "Antique Pine" varnish to the whole dresser to protect the surface.*

TEMPLATES

The templates may be resized to any scale required. They can be enlarged or reduced using a photocopier.

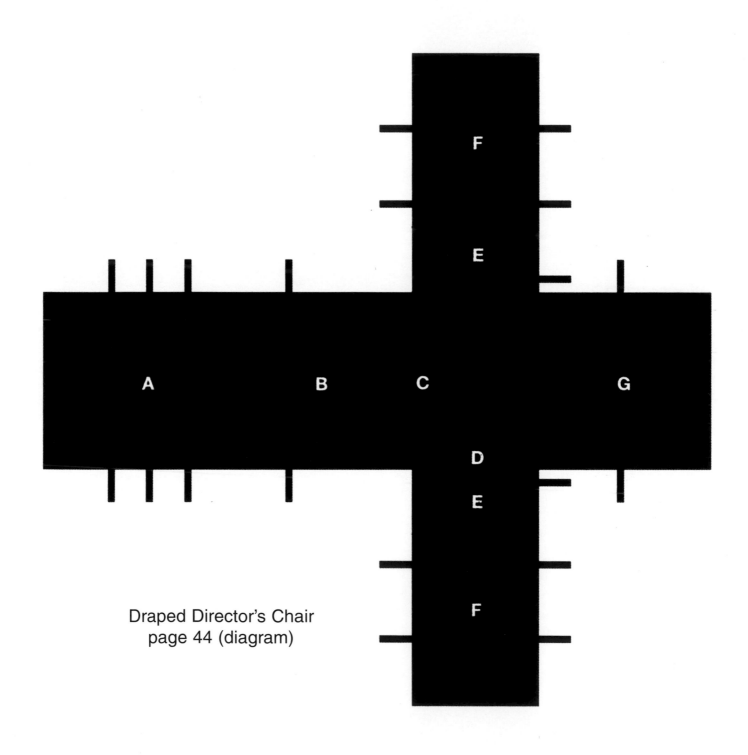

Draped Director's Chair
page 44 (diagram)

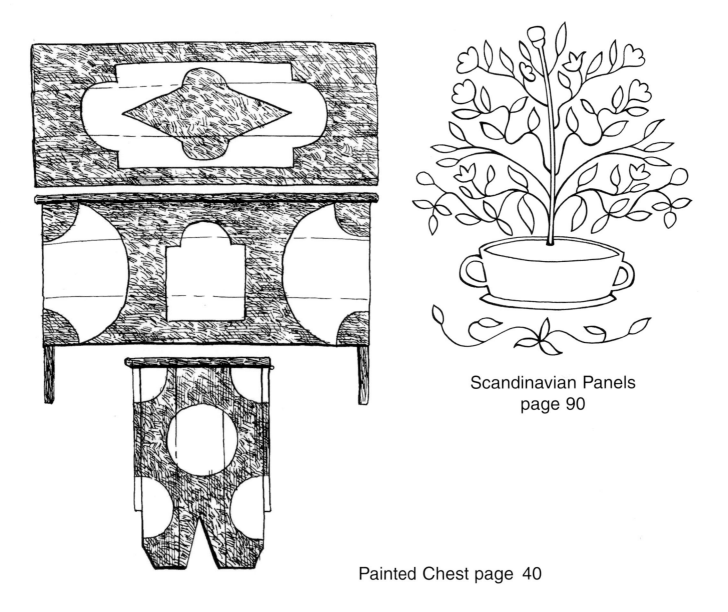

Scandinavian Panels
page 90

Painted Chest page 40

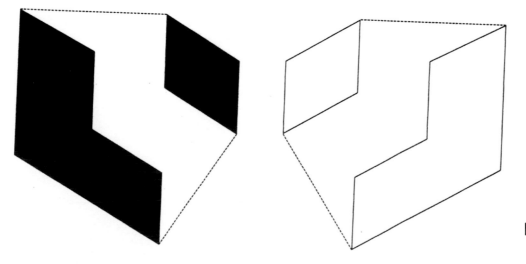

Escher's Deckchair
page 42

INDEX